COUNTRIES IN OUR WORLD

ITALY
IN OUR WORLD

Ann Weil

A+
Smart Apple Media

Published by Smart Apple Media
P.O. Box 3263, Mankato, Minnesota 56002

Printed in the United States of America at Corporate
Graphics, in North Mankato, Minnesota.

Published by arrangement with the Watts Publishing
Group LTD, London.

Library of Congress Cataloging-in-Publication Data
Weil, Ann.
  Italy in our world / by Ann Weil.
     p. cm. -- (Countries in our world)
  Includes bibliographical references and index.
  Summary: "Describes the geography, landscape,
economy, government, and culture of Italy today and
discusses Italy's influence of and relations with the rest
of the world"--Provided by publisher.
  ISBN 978-1-59920-389-8 (library binding)
  1. Italy--Juvenile literature. I. Title.
  DG417.W45 2012
  945--dc22
                         2010031860

1305
3-2011

9 8 7 6 5 4 3 2 1

Produced for Franklin Watts by
White-Thomson Publishing Ltd
Series consultant: Rob Bowden
Editor: Sonya Newland
Designer: Clare Nicholas
Picture researcher: Amy Sparks

Picture Credits
Corbis: 10 (Christiano Chiodi), 13 (David Turnley),
14 (Karen Kasmauski/Science Faction), 15 (Joyce
Ravid), 23 (Chris Helgren/Reuters), 25 (De
Renzis/epa), 27 (Marcello Paternostro/Reuters);
Dreamstime: 1 (Wh Chow), 5 (Veronika Bakos),
6 (Wh Chow), 11 (Imagestalk), 17 (Valeria Cantone),
18 (Maria Cristina Sferra), 19 (Jonatha Borzicchi),
21 (Orientaly), 24 (Fabrizio Argonauta), 26 (Britvich);
Shutterstock: Mikhail Nekrasov; **WTPix:** 7, 8, 12, 16,
20, 22, 28, 29.
Map artwork on page 4 by Stefan Chabluk.

Contents

Introducing Italy

Italy is one of the most developed countries in the world. It is a popular tourist destination and is famous for its fashion and its food. Although it is a relatively small country, its capital, Rome, was once the center of a huge empire.

BASIC DATA
Official name: **Italian Republic**
Capital: **Rome**
Size: **116,306 sq miles (301,230 sq km)**
Population: **58,090,681 (2010 est.)**
Currency: **Euro**

Where in the World?

The boot-shaped Italian peninsula in southern Europe stretches 500 miles (800 km) south into the Mediterranean Sea. In the North, the Alps Mountains form a natural boundary with France, Switzerland, Austria, and Slovenia. The rest of the country is surrounded by sea, which means Italy has thousands of miles (kilometers) of coastline. Italy also includes Sicily, Sardinia, and several smaller islands.

▶ *Italy has land borders with France, Switzerland, Austria, and Slovenia, as well as the two small countries of San Marino and Vatican City.*

Ancient Civilization

This modern, developed country has a long history. The Roman civilization began around the 10th century BC. The ancient Romans are remembered for their development of law, art, and language. This civilization gradually spread, and by the first century AD, a vast Roman Empire stretched all across Europe, North Africa, and the Near East. The Roman Empire lasted until the fifth century.

IT'S A FACT!

Two of the world's smallest countries lie completely within Italy's borders. Vatican City in Rome is the smallest country in the world at only 0.2 sq miles (0.5 sq km). San Marino, on Mount Titano in north-central Italy, is 24 sq miles (52 sq km), and is the world's fifth smallest country.

▼ *The Trevi Fountain is one of many famous landmarks in Rome, the ancient capital of the huge Roman Empire.*

Roman Remains

Remains of the Roman civilization can still be seen in all parts of the former empire, and the technology the ancient Romans developed continues to influence our modern world. The Romans built many great public buildings, including the famous Colosseum in Rome where gladiators battled each other to the death.

City-states

After the fall of the Roman Empire, some cities in Italy became powerful, independent states known as city-states. These were independently ruled, and each area developed its own sense of identity. Places

▲ *Work began on the Colosseum in Rome in 70 AD, and it was completed 10 years later. Over the centuries, earthquakes have damaged the remains.*

such as Venice, Florence, and Milan grew rich from trade with countries in Europe and Asia.

The Kingdom of Italy

Between the 15th and the 19th centuries, France, Spain, and Austria all invaded Italy and took control of different regions. Eventually the Italians won the fight against their foreign rulers, and the country was united as the Kingdom of Italy in 1861.

IT STARTED HERE

The Renaissance

After the fall of the Roman Empire in the fifth century, much of the Romans' knowledge was lost or forgotten. In the 14nth century, however, people became interested in learning and in the arts once again. This period in history became known as the Renaissance, which means "rebirth." It began in Italy and spread throughout Europe. Art, music, literature, and learning all flourished during the Renaissance.

The Sweet Life

After World War II (1939–45), Italy became a republic rather than a kingdom. It recovered more quickly from the effects of the war than many other European countries. The economy boomed and Italians enjoyed high incomes and a relaxed lifestyle known as *la dolce vita* ("the sweet life"). However, the global economic crisis that began in 2008 hit Italy harder than many other countries. This was partly because the Italian economy relied on manufacturing and exporting products, and when the crisis hit, other countries stopped buying so many Italian-made goods. A survey found that Italians were the least happy people in Western Europe.

THE HOME OF...

Coffee Culture

Coffee was introduced to Europeans around 1600 when the first shipment of coffee from the Muslim world arrived in the port city of Venice, Italy. From Italy, the fashion for drinking coffee spread throughout Europe. Today, you can order an *espresso* almost anywhere in the world. This strong-tasting coffee is made using a machine invented in Italy.

Landscapes and Environment

Most of Italy's landscape is rugged and mountainous, but there are some flat plain areas and long stretches of sandy beach along the coastline. The country is also dotted with lakes and volcanoes.

Coast and Mountains

Surrounded on three sides by the Mediterranean Sea, Italy's total coastline—including the large islands of Sicily and Sardinia—is 4,722 miles (7,600 km). In the north, the Alps separate Italy from the rest of Europe, and the Apennine Mountains run from the Alps in the north to the toe of the boot in the south, forming a kind of backbone through the country. This rugged mountain range includes Europe's southernmost glacier, the Calderone. Northern Italy experiences hot summers and cold winters. Southern Italy has even hotter summers, and winters are usually mild and rainy.

GLOBAL LEADER

World Heritage Sites
Italy has 43 World Heritage Sites— places considered to be of special cultural significance. This is more than any other country. These range from royal palaces and cathedrals to lakes, valleys, and prehistoric remains.

▼ *The island of Sardinia, famous for its beautiful beaches, lies off the west coast of Italy.*

Volcanoes

Italy is home to three very active volcanoes, which have all erupted in the last 100 years. Mount Vesuvius, in southwestern Italy, is the only active volcano in mainland Europe. Mount Etna is on the island of Sicily and is almost constantly erupting. Stromboli, on an island of the same name, has erupted many times already in the 21st century, including an eruption in August 2008.

Wildlife

Despite Italy's relatively small size, more than one-third of all European animal species can be found there. Many native animals are under threat, but efforts are being made to protect them and increase their numbers again. Some endangered animals can be found in national parks and in the dense forests in the Abruzzo region of the Apennines. A national park not far from

 The ancient city of Pompeii, buried under rock and ash after Vesuvius (in the background) erupted, has now been excavated.

IT'S A FACT!

One of the most famous volcanic disasters in history occurred in Italy in 79 AD when Vesuvius erupted. Burning ash and volcanic rock rained down on the ancient city of Pompeii. People suffocated under clouds of poisonous gases, and the entire city remained buried—and mostly forgotten—for more than 1,500 years.

Rome is home to a handful of formerly endangered species: the Apennine wolf, Marsican bear, fox, mountain goat, and Apennine lynx.

Earthquakes

Because Italy lies on two fault lines—large cracks in the rock on the Earth's surface—it has suffered from many earthquakes over the centuries. In April 2009, a huge earthquake hit the 13th-century mountain city of L'Aquila in the Abruzzo region. When the earthquake struck, the old buildings crumbled and the whole city was destroyed. Almost 300 people were killed and 68,000 more were left homeless.

Melting the Alps

Like most other countries, Italy faces a number of environmental issues. One of the most serious is the effect that global warming is having on the landscape. As temperatures rise, warmer-than-usual weather has caused glaciers to melt in the Alps on Italy's border with Switzerland. The landscape has changed so much that in 2009, Italy and Switzerland agreed to change the position of the border between the two countries.

▲ *The 2009 earthquake in the Abruzzo region was the worst to hit Italy in 30 years.*

Flooding in Venice

Another effect of global warming has been an increase in floods. Flooding has always been a problem in the Italian city of Venice, which is made up of more than 100 small islands in a marshy lagoon. Recently the floods have been much worse, though, and in December 2008, record high tides put much of the city under water, damaging many old buildings and the precious artifacts housed there.

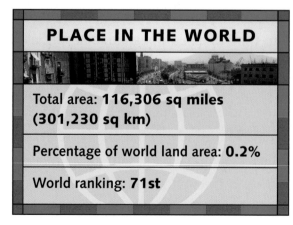

PLACE IN THE WORLD

Total area: **116,306 sq miles (301,230 sq km)**

Percentage of world land area: **0.2%**

World ranking: **71st**

Pollution

Pollution is another major environmental issue in Italy as polluting gases are released into the atmosphere by factories in the big cities. In 2006, a new way to fight pollution was introduced in several Italian cities: special pavement bricks. When exposed to light, a chemical in the bricks reacts with the poisonous gas carbon monoxide in the air, turning it into water and carbon dioxide.

▼ *Heavy traffic—such as this in Naples— contributes to air pollution in Italy.*

IT'S A FACT!

Italy is planning to reduce pollution further by encouraging people to rent environmentally friendly electric cars. As part of this "e-mobility" plan, more than 100 electric cars were made available in Rome, Milan, and Pisa in 2009, with special stations where they can be charged—the electric equivalent of gas stations.

Population and Migration

About 99 percent of Italy's population is ethnic Italian, and the country has far fewer ethnic minorities than its neighbors in Europe. There are only a few small minority groups that speak languages other than Italian.

Where Do Italians Live?

Italy has a population of just over 58 million, two-thirds of whom live in cities. In fact, Italy has the fifth highest population density in Europe. Northern Italy is more populated then the south as most of the industry is found there, and people go there in search of work. The southern part of the country, including the large island of Sicily, is more rural. The people there also tend to be poorer than those in northern Italy.

PLACE IN THE WORLD

Population: **58,090,681 (2010 est.)**

Percentage of world total: **0.9%**

World ranking: **23rd**

▼ *Italy has an aging population. Here, elderly men gather to pass the time discussing business and politics.*

Immigrants in Italy

Around 3.7 million immigrants live in Italy.
Nearly half of them come from other parts of
Europe, particularly Eastern Europe, but there
are also many from North Africa and Asia.
In some countries, immigrants have been
accepted by the native people, but in Italy,
immigrants often live in separate communities.
They keep their own customs and traditions
rather than adopting Italian culture. Some
Italians are more suspicious of immigrants
than other Europeans, and feel that they have
too many rights. Most immigrants have
settled in northern Italy, where there are more
jobs, and the fear and dislike of immigrants
by Italians is stronger here than in other parts
of the country.

▲ *Villa Literno, near Naples, was once a summer
resort. Now, immigrants from Africa live in the
old, run-down vacation apartments.*

Illegal Immigration

Although many immigrants in Italy go
through the proper channels and settle there
legally, many more arrive in the country
illegally. This is easier to do than in some other
countries, because the long coastline means it
is readily accessible by boat, and immigrants
may be able to arrive undetected by the
authorities. Many illegal immigrants come
from southeast Europe and Africa in search
of jobs and a better quality of life than they
have in their own countries.

Emigration

Southern Italy has a long history of emigration and there are now as many people with Italian heritage living outside Italy as there are in the country itself—about 60 million. From the 1870s to the 1970s, about 25 million Italians left Italy. Most were farmers from southern Italy and the island of Sicily. They left home hoping to find work elsewhere.

IT'S A FACT!

America was named after the 15th-century Italian explorer Amerigo Vespucci, who made several voyages to the Americas, and other parts of the world.

Italian-Americans

The United States was one of the most popular destinations for Italians looking for a new life. They could make more money working in America than they could at home. Although some stayed in the United States, millions took their new wealth home to Italy. Today, about 1 in 10 people in the U.S. have some Italian blood, and Italian-Americans form the fifth largest ethnic group in the U.S.

▼ *A brass band at the Feast of San Gennaro, an Italian festival celebrated in the area known as Little Italy in New York City.*

FAMOUS ITALIAN

Lee Iacocca
(b. 1924)

The son of Italian immigrants, Iacocca became one of the most famous businessmen in the world. As president of Ford Motor Company and the chairman of Chrysler Corporation, he changed the way cars were built and sold in America. He also wrote several books about his experiences that continue to inspire business people today.

Life in a New Country

There are now five million Italians living abroad. About half live in other countries of the European Union and the rest have settled mainly in the United States, South America, and Australia. Most migrants, then as now, are from the poorer south. Italian immigrants to Western Europe, North and South America, and Australia tend to adapt well to life in a new country. They are usually proud of their Italian heritage, but still adopt some of the customs and traditions of their new country. Some have become successful business people, film and TV stars, or politicians.

▲ Lee Iacocca's parents left Italy in the 1920s and settled in the United States. He is now one of America's most famous businessmen.

Culture and Lifestyles

Italian culture spread around the world during the time of the Roman Empire, and it continues to have a global influence today. Within Italy many traditions remain strong, but new ideas are coming in from other parts of the world at a faster rate than ever before.

Food

Pasta is Italy's national dish, and there are more than 100 different types. Pasta is usually served with sauces made from meat, vegetables, or cheese. Another national dish, pizza, was invented by a cook in Naples in 1775, and is now one of the most popular foods in the world. While people in many countries rely more on fast food, Italians do not want to eat and run. Enjoying meals with family and friends is part of their way of life. The Slow Food Movement began in Italy in 1986 as a reaction against this trend to eat on the go. Now, it encourages food appreciation in more than 80 countries.

IT'S A FACT!

Italian families save more money than the Japanese and Germans, and three times more than Americans.

▲ *A woman buys fish at a market. Because of its long coastline, fresh fish is readily available in Italy.*

16

Family

Italians were once known for having large families, but now Italy has one of the lowest birth rates in Europe. Italians tend to live at home longer than people in other countries. Unmarried children often live with their parents into their thirties. More than 80 percent of Italian men aged between 18 and 30 still live with their parents. The average Italian man is 33 when his first child is born, making Italian men the oldest first-time fathers in Europe.

THE HOME OF...

Bologna University

The University of Bologna, in northern Italy, is the oldest continually operating university in Europe. It was founded in 1088 and continues to enroll both Italian and international students. It ranks in the world's top 50 universities, and is known particularly for its teaching of law.

Religion

The majority of Italians (90 percent) are Catholic, and Italy has been an important center for the Roman Catholic Church for more than 1,000 years. Today, this is the world's largest Christian church, with one billion followers worldwide. The Catholic Church's base is in Vatican City, a tiny independent state surrounded by the city of Rome.

▼ *Pope Benedict XVI, leader of the Catholic Church, outside the Vatican in Rome.*

Italian Music

Music has been an important part of Italian culture since ancient times. The viol, violin, cello, and piano were all invented by Italians, and some of the world's most famous classical composers were Italian, including Giuseppe Verdi, Giacomo Puccini, and Antonio Vivaldi. Opera singers such as Luciano Pavarotti and Andrea Bocelli have a worldwide following today. Although there are Italian pop stars, such as Eros Ramazzotti, young Italians also enjoy British and American pop music, as well as music from other European countries.

▼ *Italy is considered the birthplace of opera, and La Scala in Milan is one of the most famous opera houses in the world.*

FAMOUS ITALIAN

Luciano Pavarotti (1935–2007)

Opera star Luciano Pavarotti was born to a poor family in northern Italy. He became a huge celebrity, known for his size as well as his talent. His millions of fans included many young people who did not like opera until after they saw him performing with rock stars such as Elton John, Sting, and Bono.

Soccer Crazy

Italians are passionate about sports, especially soccer. Around five million Italians play soccer regularly and there are thousands of soccer clubs throughout the country. The Italian national team has won the World Cup four times—most recently in 2006— more than any other country apart from Brazil. Many of the world's best soccer players choose to play with Italian clubs, particularly the two most successful—Juventus and Milan. Italy also sends soccer stars to other countries where they are in high demand.

▲ Fans of the soccer team AC Milan celebrate in the street. Most Italians are ardent soccer supporters.

Time to Talk

Italians own more cell phones and send more text messages per head of population than any other country. About 10,000 messages are sent from Italian cell phones every second of every day.

GLOBAL LEADER

Motor Racing

Ferrari is probably the best-known racing team in the world, and the oldest and most successful team in Formula One. Since it was established in 1948, the Ferrari team has won 14 Constructors' Championships and 14 Drivers' Championships.

Economy and Trade

In the second half of the 20th century, Italy had one of the strongest economies in the world, but when the global economic crisis struck in the early 2000s, Italy was hit hard. It struggled to keep up with other countries in the European Union and to compete in world markets.

Economic Boom

Throughout the 20th century, the Italian economy had its ups and downs. During World War II, Italy fought alongside Germany, and when they lost the war many people feared that the Italian economy would take years to recover. However, a shift in focus from farming to industry helped the Italian economy survive the hardship experienced in many other countries after the war. By 1987, the economy was as strong as that of the United Kingdom.

Economic Decline

As rapidly developing countries such as China and India became more industrialized in the early years of the 21st century, many Western nations found they could not compete with the low prices offered for products made in these countries. The economies of several Western nations, including Italy, began to decline.

PLACE IN THE WORLD

Value of economy:
US$1,821,000 million

Percentage of world total: **0.03%**

World ranking: **10th**

◀ *High unemployment in Italy resulted in many people setting up street stalls to earn a living.*

In 2007, living standards in Italy—once one of the highest in Europe—fell behind those in Spain. Unemployment began to grow, and people found it increasingly difficult to find and keep jobs. Despite this, Italy remained a rich country by global standards.

Farming

Only a quarter of Italy's land is suitable for farming, but this industry is still one of the most important in the country. It is famous for its wine and olive oil in particular, but in this area, too, Italy was overtaken by other countries in the 2000s. In 2008, a large Spanish food company bought the Italian company Bertolli, one of the world's best-known olive-oil labels. This gave the Spanish company control of half the Italian market and made it the world's leader in olive-oil sales. Some people feared that smaller Italian brands would be forced to sell out as a result of this takeover.

▼ *A farmer checks his grapes at a vineyard in Tuscany.*

IT'S A FACT!

Eight percent of Italy's farmland is used to grow organic crops. Only Australia and Argentina devote a larger proportion of available farmland to organic farming.

Tourism

Italy has been a tourist destination since at least the 16th century, and it is still one of the most popular places in the world for vacationers. People travel to Italy to visit the Roman ruins and other places of historical interest, as well as the hundreds of coastal resorts. Italy is ranked fifth in the world in tourism. Only France, Spain, the United States, and China receive more foreign tourists. Tourism accounts for three percent of Italy's gross domestic product (GDP) and employs a million people, five percent of the country's workforce.

▼ *Tourists come from all over the world to visit famous historical sites like the Leaning Tower of Pisa.*

Cars

Many of the world's most prestigious (and expensive) sports cars are Italian, including Ferrari, Lamborghini, Maserati, Bugatti, and De Tomaso. The auto industry is important to the Italian economy, as cars are one of its biggest exports. The car manufacturer Fiat is the largest in Italy, and in 2009 it merged with the American car company Chrysler. It was hoped that this merger would create a bigger market for Italian cars in the United States.

▼ *Glass-blowing on the island of Murano in Venice. The craft has been practiced here for centuries.*

Hand-made in Italy

Unlike China, where most goods are mass-produced in large factories, many Italian products are still custom-made by small, family-owned businesses. Clothing, ceramics, and glassware are often produced by skilled craftsmen and exported all over the world.

IT STARTED HERE

Glass-blowing

Some of the world's finest glass comes from Italy, where the process of glass-blowing originated on Murano, an island in the Venetian lagoon. Venetian glass is now much sought-after. These unique items are beautiful and expensive.

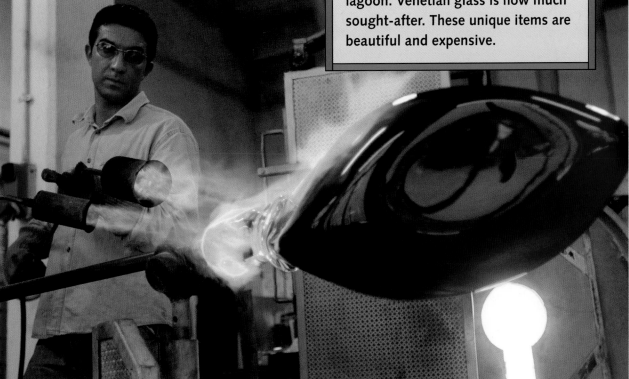

Italy is a republic, which means that it is not ruled by a king or queen, but by representatives elected by the Italian people. There are many political parties, and the government changes frequently.

Government Organization

Until the end of World War II, Italy was ruled by a king. In 1946, the Italian people voted to abolish the monarchy and become a republic. The following year, a constitution was established. Italy now has a president, Giorgio Napolitano, and a prime minister, Silvio Berlusconi. Unlike the U.S., where the president is the head of government, the president of Italy is only a ceremonial figure. The prime minister is the head of government and runs the country.

FAMOUS ITALIAN

Silvio Berlusconi (b. 1936)

The Italian prime minister, Silvio Berlusconi, is a self-made billionaire and the richest man in Italy. As well as being elected prime minister three times, he heads a media empire and owns AC Milan—one of the world's best soccer clubs. Although he has been put on trial for corruption several times, he has always been cleared of the charges.

◀ *Italian prime minister Silvio Berlusconi speaks at a rally in Turin during his 2008 election campaign.*

Italy and the European Union

Although Italy was one of the founders of the European Union, its relationship with other EU members has not always been good. In 2003, there were protests all over the country when Italy joined with the United Kingdom and Spain in supporting the U.S. invasion of Iraq. Germany and France, traditionally allies of Italy, were against the invasion. In 2008, Italy rebelled against the EU's climate-change goals. The Italian prime minister argued that the plans were too expensive and that Italy could not afford to meet the goals. The following year, the prime minister threatened to veto the EU Energy and Climate Package.

IT'S A FACT!

Italy is among the worst-performing states in the Climate Change Performance Index, which ranks countries according to their emissions and how well they are meeting climate-change targets.

▼ *Italy chose to support the U.S.-led invasion of Iraq in 2003. Italian troops remained in Iraq until 2006.*

▶ *Northern cities are filled with shops selling expensive designer items, and the people who live there have money to spend. In the south, it's a different story.*

North and South

The division of Italy into the more prosperous north and the poorer south is a source of tension within the country. Generally, Italians in the north of the country have a lot more money than those in the south. The gross domestic product per person is almost three times higher in the richest northern areas, such as Bologna and Milan, than in the south. Southern Italy includes eight regions with 35 percent of the population, but is largely underdeveloped. Many of the people who live there have a hard life.

Women in Italy

In the 1970s, Italian women won the right to divorce their husbands, and in 2001 Italy had more female business managers and administrators than any other country.

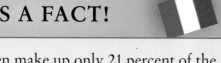

IT'S A FACT!

Women make up only 21 percent of the members of parliament in Italy, making it 52nd in the world rankings. European nations such as Spain and Germany have percentages in the 30s. Fifty-six percent of Rwanda's parliament is women—the most of any country.

Now, though, it seems that feminism is out of fashion. Italian television has been accused of promoting sexism with game shows that feature attractive women in bikinis. Many people blame the prime minister, Silvio Berlusconi, for this trend because he owns the television networks. Italy also now has the lowest percentage of working women in Europe, and women hold only two percent of top management positions.

GOING GLOBAL

Due to emigration from Italy in the late 19th and early 20th centuries, there are now mafia groups in several countries, including the United States, Canada, and Australia. Although these groups, or "families," are usually independent of one another, they have similar structures and codes of conduct.

The Mafia

The mafia is a large criminal organization that is believed to have begun on the Italian island of Sicily in the late 19th century. The mafia controls many businesses and large farming operations, as well as the trade in illegal drugs. In the past, Italian politicians and judges have even been linked to the mafia. Although many mafia suspects have been arrested since the 1980s, the mafia is still big business in Italy, especially in the south, and mafia groups also exist in many other countries.

◀ *Mafia boss Bernardo Provenzano was arrested in 2006, but the organization continues in Italy and around the world.*

Italy in 2020

Although it is a relatively wealthy country by international standards, Italy faces several problems. These must be addressed in the next few years in order to improve the economy and the quality of life for the Italian people, particularly in the south.

Settling Debts

Italy's public debt is the third highest of all the world's industrialized countries. This has put pressure on the economy, which may become worse in the future. It may be a particular problem for future generations if the population continues to age and there are fewer people working and paying taxes. The number of retired people compared to those in employment is on the rise. At 28 percent in 2006, it was the second highest in the world. Unless there is a baby boom, that ratio is expected to double by 2040. To address this problem, Italy may have to encourage more immigrants to fill the labor gap.

GLOBAL LEADER

Healthcare

Italy has a national healthcare system, in which healthcare is free to all Italian citizens. The World Health Organization recently rated Italy's healthcare system as the second best in the world after France.

▼ *Italy needs a baby boom to address the problem of its aging population.*

Getting Ahead

To be elected to government in Italy, a person has to be at least 40 years old, and there is no maximum age. Because there are so many political parties with many different ideas, it can be hard for young, educated Italians to get ahead if their political ideas are different from those in power. More than half of all university graduates admitted they would like to work in a country where advancement is based on ability, not politics. The government may have to rethink such policies if it wants to encourage young people to stay in Italy.

▲ *These young people are earning money by playing music in the street. It can be hard for young people to establish good careers in Italy.*

Environmental Issues

By 2020, Italy will need to have seriously addressed its environmental problems. While many countries are reducing their greenhouse-gas emissions, Italy's have risen in the past 20 years. The goals set by the Kyoto Protocol may encourage Italy to work harder at reducing emissions and pollution. The country may also turn more to renewable energy sources to meet its needs. Italy is likely to double its capacity target for expanding the use of wind energy as it aims to meet EU goals for boosting renewable power.

IT'S A FACT!

Italy generated about 3.5 billion kilowatt hours of electricity on wind farms in 2006 —equal to about one percent of total power demand. That's enough to meet the needs of over 4.5 million Italians.

Glossary

constitution a document that lays out the main laws of a nation; laws are not allowed to be passed that contradict a country's constitution.

economy the financial system of a country or region, including how much money is made from the production and sale of goods and services.

emigration when someone leaves the country of their birth to settle in another country.

emissions gases that are given off during industrial processes or by vehicles.

ethnic group a group of people classed together according to their racial, national, linguistic, or cultural origin or background.

export to send or transport products or materials abroad for sale or trade.

feminism a strong belief that women should have the same rights and opportunities as men.

glacier a large mass of ice that moves very slowly down a mountain valley.

gladiators men who entertained the public by fighting each other or wild animals in ancient Roman times.

global warming the gradual rise in temperatures on the surface of the earth, caused by changes in the amount of greenhouse gases in the atmosphere.

greenhouse gas a gas that helps trap warmth in the atmosphere, which can contribute to global warming if too much is generated on earth.

gross domestic product (GDP) the total amount of money a country earns every year.

immigrant a person who has moved from another country to live.

lagoon a large pool of seawater.

Muslim a follower of the Islamic religion.

peninsula a large mass of land that juts out into a body of water.

pollution ruining the environment with man-made waste such as vehicle emissions, waste gases from factories, or chemicals from fertilizers.

population density the number of people living in a square mile or square kilometer of a country.

Renaissance a revival of learning and culture that began in Italy in the fourteenth century and lasted until the seventeenth century.

republic a system of government in which people elect officials to make decisions on their behalf, rather than being ruled by a king or queen.

rural relating to the countryside.

sexism a belief that people of the opposite sex are inferior.

veto to vote against something.

Further Information

Books

Celebrate Italy
Celebrate
by Robyn Hardyman
(Chelsea Clubhouse, 2009)

Focus on Italy
World in Focus
by Jen Green
(World Almanac Library, 2007)

Italy
Living In…
by Ruth Thomson
(Sea-to-Sea Publications, 2007)

A Visit to Italy
A Visit To
by Rachael Bell
(Heinemann Library, 2008)

Web Sites

www.italiantourism.com
This is the official Italian tourist information site, with maps and information on Italy.

www.travelforkids.com/Funtodo/Italy/italy.htm
Take a journey through Italy with this fun site, travelling from Rome to Pompeii.

http://europa.eu/europago/welcome.jsp and http://europa.eu/youth
These European Union sites have been set up especially for children and young people.

https://www.cia.gov/library/publications/the-world-factbook/geos/it.html
The CIA World Factbook entry on Italy. Gives statistics and information on the land, people, government, and economy of Italy.

Every effort has been made by the publisher to ensure that these web sites contain no inappropriate or offensive material. However, because of the nature of the Internet, it is impossible to guarantee that the content of these sites will not be altered. We strongly advise that Internet access is supervised by a responsible adult.

Index

Numbers in **bold** indicate pictures